ECHOES FROM THE ICE

One Girl's Antarctic Quest to Hear What the Planet Is Telling Us

WENDI PILLARS

COPYRIGHT © 2025 BY WENDI PILLARS

ALL RIGHTS RESERVED.

NO PORTION OF THIS BOOK MAY BE REPRODUCED IN ANY FORM WITHOUT WRITTEN PERMISSION FROM THE PUBLISHER OR AUTHOR, EXCEPT AS PERMITTED BY U.S. COPYRIGHT LAW.

THIS PUBLICATION IS DESIGNED TO PROVIDE ACCURATE AND AUTHORITATIVE INFORMATION IN REGARD TO THE SUBJECT MATTER COVERED. IT IS SOLD WITH THE UNDERSTANDING THAT NEITHER THE AUTHOR NOR THE PUBLISHER IS ENGAGED IN RENDERING LEGAL, INVESTMENT, ACCOUNTING OR OTHER PROFESSIONAL SERVICES. WHILE THE PUBLISHER AND AUTHOR HAVE USED THEIR BEST EFFORTS IN PREPARING THIS BOOK, THEY MAKE NO REPRESENTATIONS OR WARRANTIES WITH RESPECT TO THE ACCURACY OR COMPLETENESS OF THE CONTENTS OF THIS BOOK AND SPECIFICALLY DISCLAIM ANY IMPLIED WARRANTIES OF MERCHANTABILITY OR FITNESS FOR A PARTICULAR PURPOSE. NO WARRANTYMAY BE CREATED OR EXTENDED BY SALES REPRESENTATIVES OR WRITTEN SALES MATERIALS. THE ADVICE AND STRATEGIES CONTAINED HEREIN MAY NOT BE SUITABLE FOR YOUR SITUATION. YOU SHOULD CONSULT WITH A PROFESSIONAL WHEN APPROPRIATE. NEITHER THE PUBLISHER NOR THE AUTHOR SHALL BE LIABLE FOR ANY LOSS OF PROFIT OR ANY OTHER COMMERCIAL DAMAGES, INCLUDING BUT NOT LIMITED TO SPECIAL, INCIDENTAL, CONSEQUENTIAL, PERSONAL, OR OTHER DAMAGES.

1ST EDITION 2025
ISBN: 978-1-970487-00-8 (PAPERBACK)
ISBN: 978-1-970487-01-5 (HARDCOVER)

This one's for you, Mom.

For you, Mom, who gave me roots, courageous wings, and a compass.
And to Ian, who reminds me why stories--and ice--still matter.

At the frozen edges of the Earth, where ancient ice holds the stories of a changing planet, Alexandra sets out on an unforgettable journey. In Antarctica's dynamic wilderness, she listens closely to the whispers of melting glaciers, shifting climate, and the choices that will shape our future. This inspiring adventure combines real science with courage and curiosity, inviting young readers and educators alike to explore the power of one voice to understand and protect our world.

THE ISLAND SKY

The streets of Ushuaia smelled of salt and woodsmoke, the air crisp with the promise of winter. Alexandra tightened her grip on her backpack as she followed her Aunt Claudia, one of the ship's favorite expedition leaders, through the bustling port, past crates of supplies and crews making last-minute preparations.

"There she is," Claudia said, nodding ahead.

Alexandra's breath caught as she looked up at the sleek white and blue ship. The Island Sky rocked gently at the dock, ropes creaking, black-browed albatrosses soaring overhead. It may have been the smallest ship at the dock, but it still looked imposing—built for adventure, capable of navigating spaces that larger ships couldn't reach. It seemed sturdy, serious, and ready to take on the wild, frozen world ahead.

"Still sure about this?" Claudia asked, watching her niece's face.

Alexandra swallowed hard, then nodded. "More than ever."

Claudia grinned. "Good. Because Antarctica doesn't just let anyone in. You have to earn it. And that's all part of what we call "Plan A."

Alexandra tilted her head. "What about Plan B?"

"There isn't one," she replied with a smile. "That's why people like us come here, to listen, to learn, and maybe…to tell the story before it's too late."

"Tell the story?"

"You'll see." Claudia winked. "Just pay attention. The ice has a lot to say."

As Alexandra took her first step up the gangway, a sudden gust of wind curled around her, colder than the rest. She shivered, but not from the chill.

For the briefest moment, she had the strangest feeling—like something unseen had stirred at the edge of her thoughts, watching, waiting. She shook it off. Probably just nerves.

Her parents were halfway across the world, posted overseas for work. When Aunt Claudia had invited her on this expedition, it had been perfect timing; her school was on break, and she wouldn't just be stuck waiting at home. She'd be doing something important.

At school, Antarctica had always been a place at the edges of the map, a vast white mystery too far away to feel real. And now she was about to explore the Antarctic Peninsula, thanks to her aunt.

She pressed a hand against her notebook, tucked safely inside her jacket, right over her heart. She would write it all down. Draw it. Capture everything, because when she came back, she knew she would have a story to tell.

As Alexandra looked out over the endless sea, something strange happened. The wind shifted and for half a second, it sounded like a whisper. She blinked. Had the wind just said…*listen*?

Crossing The Drake Passage

Alexandra leaned against the ship's railing, the icy wind whipping her cheeks. The horizon seemed endless, a blur of steel-gray waves capped with frothy white foam. Claudia stood beside her, both hands firmly gripping the rail.

"This," Claudia said with a smile, "is the Drake Passage. One of the wildest stretches of water on Earth."

Alexandra's stomach fluttered—not just from the rolling waves but from excitement. "Why is it so wild?", she asked.

Claudia motioned toward the heaving waves. "You're standing at the gateway to Antarctica. This is where the Atlantic, Pacific, and Southern Oceans meet, and they don't always get along. The winds here are the strongest in the world, and the currents are like rivers within the ocean, constantly clashing and swirling."

Alexandra's eyes widened and she held on tighter as the ship rolled with the swell of a giant wave. "So, it's like the ocean's battle zone?"

"Exactly," Claudia said with a grin. "But there's more to it. The Drake Passage is the only connection between the Southern Ocean and the rest of the world's oceans. It's like a bridge—or maybe a giant funnel—where water, currents, and even marine life pass through to keep the planet in balance."

Alexandra tightened her scarf against the cold. "What kind of marine life?"

"Oh, everything from krill—tiny creatures that fuel the food web here—to whales, seals, and seabirds like albatrosses. Some of the creatures we'll see on this trip only exist because the Drake Passage connects the ecosystems of Antarctica to the rest of the world."

Alexandra thought about this for a moment, as the ship rocked beneath their feet. "So, without the Drake Passage, Antarctica would be… cut off?"

"That's right," Claudia said. "It's more than just a wild stretch of ocean. It's like a lifeline, carrying nutrients and life to and from Antarctica. And for sailors like us, it's a rite of passage, literally and figuratively. Surviving the Drake is a badge of honor."

Alexandra smiled, her curiosity turning to determination. "Well, I guess I'd better earn mine!"

Claudia laughed, placing a reassuring hand on Alexandra's shoulder. "That's the spirit! Just keep your eyes on the horizon and your sense of adventure wide open. This is the kind of experience that stays with you forever."

As Alexandra admired the watery expanse, Claudia leaned down and whispered, "Do you know who protects this land? The Ice Guardian."

Alexandra's eyes widened. "Who's that?" she asked.

Claudia smiled mysteriously, "A spirit of the ice, watching over Antarctica and guiding those who truly care for it."

Iceberg Alley

Alexandra woke to the gentle hum of the ship and a strange, silvery glow filtering through her porthole. She scrambled out of bed, threw on her coat, and rushed outside—only to stop dead in her tracks.

They had drifted into Iceberg Alley.

Towering icebergs, some as big as city blocks, floated in the misty morning light. Some were smooth and rounded, others jagged like castle ruins, infused with so many shades of blue, as if part of an icy fashion show. The air smelled crisp and salty, and the water around them shimmered with ghostly blue and gray reflections.

A deep, thunderous BOOM echoed across the water. Alexandra gasped as a massive chunk of ice broke away from a towering iceberg and crashed into the sea, sending ripples across the surface. "Whoa!" she breathed. "Why did it just explode like that?"

"That's called calving," Dr. Harper, the ship's marine biologist, explained. "It happens when an iceberg becomes unstable and a piece breaks off. Some are gentle, but others, well, let's just say you wouldn't want to be too close." She winked.

Alexandra grinned. "It's like the iceberg is shedding its skin."
Dr. Harper nodded. "Exactly! And did you notice the color of the ice?"
Alexandra turned her eyes back to the towering glacier, now a brilliant shade of electric blue. "Yeah! Why does it look so blue?"

Dr. Harper leaned on the railing. "That's ancient ice, thousands of years old. It's been so tightly compressed over time that all the tiny air bubbles have been squeezed out. That means when sunlight hits it, only blue light escapes since it has the shortest wavelength. That's why fresh, compacted ice glows like that!"

Alexandra wrote thoughtfully in her notebook. "So, it's kind of like looking into the past?"

Dr. Harper grinned. "In a way, yes. Some icebergs even trap tiny air pockets from thousands of years ago. If you could capture that air, you'd literally be breathing in a piece of history."

Just then, the ship glided past an iceberg with strange, twisting tunnels running through it. Sunlight filtered through in dazzling shades of turquoise and silver. Alexandra wondered where it had come from.

Dr. Harper must have read her mind. "Most of these icebergs broke away from glaciers in the Weddell Sea," she said, gesturing toward the icy expanse. "That's on the eastern side of the Antarctic Peninsula, where some of the strongest winds and currents in the world send them drifting north. Some even travel past South Georgia Island, more than a thousand miles away! They can float for years before finally melting into the sea."

Alexandra squinted. Was something moving inside the iceberg's turquoise tunnel?

A flicker of light danced deep within the ice, then disappeared. She blinked.

It was probably just the sunlight.

…Or maybe it was something else.

Had the Ice Guardian just winked at her?

Alexandra And The Ocean's Secret

Bundled tightly in her orange parka, Alexandra steadied herself on the ship's deck, her breath curling into the icy Antarctic air. Below, the ocean stretched endlessly, dark and mysterious, its surface dotted with floating ice that sparkled like scattered diamonds in the weak sunlight.

Aunt Claudia stepped up beside her, a steaming mug of hot chocolate in hand. She followed Alexandra's gaze. "See that water?" she asked, nodding toward the rippling waves. "It's not just cold. It's doing something incredible."

Alexandra squinted at the sea. "Like what?"

Claudia smiled. "Remember how I told you about how the oceans meet and the currents are like rivers within the ocean, constantly clashing and swirling? Well, the Southern Ocean has a hidden superpower. It's also like a giant conveyor belt beneath the surface, moving water—and life—all around the planet."

"A conveyor belt? In the ocean?"

"That's right," Claudia said. "This is one of the windiest, stormiest places on Earth. Those powerful winds churn up nutrients from the deep, feeding everything from tiny krill to massive whales. But even more importantly, the cold, salty water here sinks to the ocean floor, setting huge currents in motion, currents that connect every ocean on the planet."

Leaning on the railing, Claudia continued. "When ocean water freezes into ice, it forces out the salt, leaving behind water that's even saltier and colder than before. This extra-salty, extra-cold water becomes really dense, kind of like syrup compared to regular water. Because it's so heavy, it sinks straight to the bottom of the ocean, like syrup settling at the bottom of a glass."

Alexandra's eyes widened. "So, all that heavy water sinking here in Antarctica is actually moving the ocean?"

"Exactly!" Claudia nodded. "As it sinks, it spreads out along the ocean floor, traveling like a slow, invisible river. It creeps through the deep sea, carrying oxygen and nutrients with it. Eventually, that water rises again in different parts of the world, bringing deep-sea nutrients up to feed marine life. This whole process helps regulate the Earth's climate, too."

Alexandra gripped the railing, her mind racing. "So, Antarctica isn't just a frozen wilderness, it's like the heart of the ocean, pumping water all over the planet."

Claudia beamed. "That's a perfect way to put it."

Alexandra stared out at the endless waves, imagining powerful currents swirling beneath the surface, connecting oceans, and feeding creatures she couldn't even see. It was a secret world, hidden in the depths.

"I'm going to remember this," she said, pulling out her notebook and adding to her thoughts from earlier in the day.

Claudia gave her a proud smile. "Good. And maybe one day, you'll help protect it."

That night, as Alexandra lay in her bunk, the ship's gentle rocking felt like the rhythm of the ocean itself. In her dreams, she heard the Ice Guardian, its voice whispering through the waves: *"Even the smallest actions create ripples in the great currents of the world."*

Humpback Encounter

As the ship glided through icy waters beyond the polar front, once known as the Antarctic Convergence, Alexandra stood near the deck's edge, breathing in the frigid air, eyes sparkling with delight. She scanned the vast, gray sea for any sign of the ocean conveyor belt. Everything was still, except for the distant crack of shifting ice. Somewhere below, far beneath the surface, she imagined the cold currents Claudia had described, flowing like slow, steady rivers in the dark.

Then– WHOOSH!

A towering column of mist shot into the sky, followed by a sleek humpback whale, its dark back arching in slow motion as it rose from the water.

Alexandra's heart leapt into her throat. "Did you SEE that?!", she practically shouted. "A WHAAALE!!!"

Down on the lower deck, a group of naturalists erupted into gasps and cheers, cameras snapping. "Humpback! Right alongside us!", one called.

The whale's enormous head lifted slowly above the surface, spyhopping, as if inspecting the ship and its tiny human passengers. It was so close, Alexandra could see–and almost count!-the barnacles encrusting its knobby head. She could see *its eye*.

"It's looking at us," she whispered, barely breathing. Alexandra couldn't speak. The whale exhaled a great, misty breath that sounded like wind through a tunnel. Or maybe…something more. She thought of the wind on the first day, the whisper she might have imagined. *Listen.*

Claudia stepped up beside her and murmured, "These whales were nearly wiped out by whalers, but they're making a comeback. They're always incredible to see, but this close? Wow."

Another naturalist added, "At one point, nearly 98% of Antarctic humpbacks were gone. Industrial whaling almost erased them from these waters, along with decimating populations of other whale species, too."

Alexandra's stomach twisted. She had read about whaling with ships hunting whales for their oil, which once lit lamps and fueled industry, but 98%? How could creatures so vast, so powerful, have been nearly erased? She had to ask,"And who were the whalers? How could they do something like that?"

Claudia nodded grimly. "In the 1930s, whalers killed nearly 30,000 humpbacks in just one season. The Southern Ocean became a kind of graveyard. The whalers came from all over," Claudia said. "Mostly Norwegians at first. Tough men, some barely older than you, who came here for adventure, money, or just because it was the only work they could find. They lived in harsh conditions out here in the cold, carving up whales day and night. Some stayed for years. Others couldn't stand it and left after a single season. For many it was good money, though, enough to buy a house in spite of the work being grueling, dangerous, and relentless."

"But after the hunting stopped, the whales slowly started coming back", she added.

Alexandra imagined it, young men, bundled in wool, their faces windburned and hands raw, hauling ropes and gutting whales, in such treacherous conditions.

The whale lingered peacefully, mesmerizing with its massive eye just above the surface. Alexadra wondered--could it remember? Did these whales somehow know what had happened here?

Another naturalist whispered, "Humpbacks are the ocean's great travelers. Some swim more than 10,000 miles every year, from tropical breeding grounds to Antarctica's icy feast. Just imagine that journey!"

Alexandra couldn't stop staring. This wasn't just a fun fact in a book. This was real. A living, breathing giant of the sea, close enough to touch.

Claudia grinned. "Looks like we're not the only explorers out here."

The whale lingered a moment longer, then, with one final breathy exhale, it arched its back once more, flaunted its enormous fluke, and slipped beneath the waves, disappearing into the blue.

Alexandra stayed at the railing long after, her mind spinning. Humpbacks could sing songs heard hundreds of miles away. They protected each other from orcas. They remembered feeding spots from decades past. How many other incredible creatures were down there, just out of sight? And just how much did they know?

The Living Ice

Alexandra's heart was still racing in disbelief from the whale encounter, gasping as she wiped emotional tears from her eyes. The humpback was drifting toward something even bigger, a towering wall of ice that loomed over the sea, its jagged edges glowing blue in the late afternoon light.

Claudia joined her, arms crossed against the cold. "That," she said, "is a glacier."

Alexandra squinted through her binoculars at the ice. Up close, it wasn't just white. Streaks of black and brown ran through it, from the rock and dirt carried down the mountain over centuries. And here and there, patches of red clung to the surface.

"Is that… blood?" Alexandra asked, half-joking.

Claudia chuckled. "Not quite. That's glacier algae. It blooms in the summer when there's enough sunlight. Some people call it 'watermelon snow' because it even smells a little sweet."

Alexandra wrinkled her nose. "Algae growing on ice? That's weird."

"It is," Claudia agreed. "But it's important. When algae grow on the surface of glaciers, they help absorb sunlight and trap heat, speeding up the melting process. That runoff feeds tiny creatures in the water, forming part of the food web. Even glaciers have life."

Alexandra ran her hands along the railing, taking it all in. The glacier wasn't just frozen—it was alive, shifting, changing, and carrying the past with it. The ice stretched for miles, an ancient, frozen river of time that had witnessed centuries of Earth's history.

A deep, low groan rumbled through the ship's hull.

Alexandra jumped. "What was that?"

Claudia pointed toward a chunk of ice, about the size of a couch, drifting nearby. "That's a growler."

Alexandra raised an eyebrow. "Because it… growls?"

"Exactly. When bits of ice scrape against the ship, trapped air bubbles pop, and it makes that eerie sound."

Alexandra watched the ice bobbing in the waves. "So, if that's a growler, then what's a bergy bit?" Claudia blinked. "Whoa! Where'd you hear that phrase?"

Alexandra hesitated. The words had come to her so easily, like she'd known them before. "I… I guess I overheard the scientists talking in Iceberg Alley."

Claudia smiled. "Ah, likely so. A bergy bit is bigger than a growler but not quite an iceberg. Kind of like an in-between stage."

Alexandra grinned. "So, baby icebergs?"

"Something like that," Claudia said with a chuckle. "But even baby icebergs can be dangerous if you're not paying attention."

Alexandra looked out at the glacier again, remembering the icebergs she'd seen in Iceberg Alley. "So, when the glacier loses a chunk of ice, that's what makes the big icebergs and baby icebergs, right?"

Claudia smiled. "Exactly. Remember that calving is what we call those chunks of ice breaking off from glaciers, crashing into the water, and floating away as icebergs. And right now, that's happening more and more.

As glaciers melt, they release massive amounts of freshwater into the sea, causing sea levels to rise and make those ocean currents change course. Icebergs, on the other hand, don't cause sea levels to rise because they're already floating in the water."

Alexandra frowned. "So, the glaciers are the real problem? I'm not quite sure I understand."

"Problem is a complicated word. Some scientists call them 'ice guardians' because they hold massive amounts of frozen water, helping regulate sea levels, ocean currents, and even the climate. But there's something else, too—when all that freshwater melts into the ocean, it changes the salinity, or how salty the water is. That can mess with the marine life, and also the ocean currents that carry warm and cold water around the planet."

"Oh, the ocean conveyor belts?", Alexandra asked, her forehead creasing.

Claudia nodded. "Yes! Some currents, like the Gulf Stream, keep places like Europe warmer than they should be. But if too much freshwater dilutes the salty ocean water, those currents could slow down or even stop. That would change weather patterns everywhere—more heat waves, stronger storms, and colder winters in some places."

Alexandra shivered, but not from the cold. "Like… places where people live?"

"More than you might think. Some coastal towns, like Charleston, South Carolina, are already seeing more flooding. And island nations like the Maldives are at risk of disappearing entirely. Even places like Bangladesh are facing stronger storms and floods because melting glaciers are changing ocean currents and weather patterns."

Alexandra swallowed, her mind spinning with the idea of this "ice guardian" quietly holding such incredible power. She'd visited Charleston once, walking along the old cobblestone streets near the harbor. Now, it seemed impossible that something so far away could have such an impact.

The glacier was like an ancient protector, slowly giving up its strength and secrets, one piece at a time. What happened if -when?- they disappeared?

Claudia leaned against the railing. "It's not just the shifting currents and rising waters. Warmer temperatures can also harm the creatures living in the ocean and disrupt entire ecosystems. You will learn about some of the most important organisms a little later, like krill which are affected by this. If their populations shrink, it affects the entire food chain, since seals, penguins, and even whales, depend on them."

Alexandra's stomach twisted. "So, melting glaciers don't just change the water. They change EVERYTHING."

Claudia nodded. "The ocean is all connected. A change in one place ripples across the world and it's not just the creatures in the water. The ice is changing, too."

Alexandra's breath caught. She was certain she had heard those words before. Was it a whisper from the Ice Guardian?

She looked out at the glacier again, its streaks of red, black, and blue telling stories older than she could imagine. It was a living record of history, constantly shifting, cracking, and breaking apart. Every change seemed to reveal a new layer of secrets, like an ancient guardian whose purpose was far beyond her understanding.

A deep crack echoed across the bay as a piece of ice broke free, crashing into the water below.

Alexandra held her breath.

The glacier wasn't just ice; it was a force of nature, alive with both history and mystery, watching over the land like a silent protector.

Discovering Tiny Giants

On the deck, Alexandra leaned into the wind, her cheeks stinging from the cold, as the ship's scientists lowered a fine-meshed net into the icy water. A few minutes later, they hauled it up, shimmering with thousands of tiny, wriggling creatures.

"Krill!" one researcher shouted excitedly

Alexandra peered closer. The swarm looked like tiny, glassy shrimp, their bodies glowing faintly pink. One flailed its legs like it was trying to swim through the air.

Dr. Harper grinned as she scooped up a handful for Alexandra to see. "These little giants are the powerhouses of Antarctica. Almost every animal here depends on them as Claudia has told you. Whales, seals, penguins, and even seabirds eat them. If krill disappeared, the entire ecosystem would collapse."

Alexandra carefully picked up a single krill, smaller than her pinky finger, about 5 cm long, yet Dr. Harper had just called it a 'giant.'

"Wait," Alexandra said, frowning. "They're so tiny. How can they be giants?"

Dr. Harper laughed. "I know, right? But krill exist in such massive swarms that together, they make up one of the largest biomasses on Earth. There are literally trillions of them in the Southern Ocean! And they're not just food; krill actually rely on the sea ice, too. Young krill feed on the algae that grow beneath it, and the ice gives them shelter from predators. But as the ice shrinks, they lose both their food and their hiding places."

Alexandra watched as the krill wiggled in her hand, its huge black eyes scanning the world. "They even glow in the dark," Dr. Harper added. "They have special bioluminescent organs that help them blend in with the shimmering light from above, hiding them from predators below."

Alexandra's mind raced. One krill was small. But together? They fed the entire ocean. "They're like stars in the sea."

"Exactly."

As she gently returned the krill to the water, Marcus, another scientist, held up a jar with a different creature, its thick, clear body glowing faintly with a red circle at its center. "We're also finding more salps lately," he said, his brow furrowed. "Too many."

Alexandra looked closer. The salps pulsed gently, filtering the water as it moved. "What are they?"

"They filter the water like krill do for their food," Marcus explained, "but unlike krill, they don't provide nutrition for the whales or penguins the same way. And as the ocean warms, salps are thriving while krill struggle."

Alexandra frowned. "So warming water could break the whole food chain?"

Dr. Harper's tone grew serious. "That's the problem. Krill need cold, nutrient-rich water to survive. If the ocean gets too warm, we'll see fewer krill and more salps. Less krill, fewer penguins. Fewer whales. It's all connected."

Frowning, Alexandra asked, "But why is the ocean getting warmer?"

Dr. Harper sighed. "It's like the Earth is getting a little too hot. The air around the planet is made up of gases, like carbon dioxide, that trap heat. Normally, some of the sun's heat escapes back into space. But with more of these gases in the air, they hold onto that heat, kind of like putting a lid on a pot of soup. The more heat that stays in, the warmer things get—including the ocean. And when the ocean gets too warm, it can hurt creatures like krill that need cold water to survive."

Alexandra looked at the tiny krill, then at the salp drifting in Marcus' jar. Two creatures, two futures.

"So, if we help the krill, we're helping the whole food chain?" she asked.

"Exactly," Dr. Harper said. "The less pollution we put into the air, the better chance krill and the entire food web—including the humpback we saw—have to survive. That means using energy more wisely, finding better ways to travel, and switching to power sources that don't create as much pollution, like wind and solar energy."

Alexandra pulled out her notebook, added some sketches then scribbled: **Small things make big things possible. Krill and cool water = survival.**

As she wrote, a chill swept over her, not from the wind, but from somewhere else. For just a second, the ship creaked in a strange way, and she thought she heard it again. A whisper on the wind.

"Notice what others miss."

She looked up, scanning the horizon and the ship's deck, but there was no one there, just endless sea and the silent sky. She pressed her hand over her notebook. She didn't know what it meant yet, but she was listening.

The Antarctic Treaty

That evening, the crew, sipping on mugs of hot chocolate, gathered in the ship's lounge where the walls were lined with colorful maps, photos of polar animals, and notes from past expeditions. The room buzzed with quiet energy, the kind that comes from people who know they're part of something bigger than themselves.

As Claudia, Alexandra, and Dr. Harper moved to the map table, Alexandra's eyes landed on the emblem on Dr. Harper's mug, a bold letter "A" and what looked like a whale fluke and seabird curling through it.

"What's that?" Alexandra asked, nodding toward the mug's design.

Dr. Harper glanced down and smiled. "Oh this? It's from the Antarctic Rights Alliance. Ever heard of it?"

Alexandra shook her head.

"We're not just here to explore," Claudia said, her voice full of quiet purpose. "We're here to protect."

Alexandra leaned in, intrigued. "What do you mean?"

Claudia unfolded a huge, weathered map of Antarctica, tracing its vast, icy expanse with her finger. "Let me tell you about the Antarctic Treaty first. It's a special agreement that countries from all over the world signed. Signed in 1959 and put into action in 1961, it's more than just a treaty. It's a promise. Countries from all over the world agreed to protect this land, to keep it peaceful and wild."

Dr. Harper, who had been quietly listening, stepped forward. "One of the most remarkable parts? Even though some countries claimed slices of Antarctica, the treaty freezes those claims literally and legally. It's called putting them in 'abeyance.' That way, no one owns Antarctica. Everyone works together and shares responsibility."

"So, some countries say they own parts of it, but the treaty makes sure no one actually does?" Alexandra asked, trying to picture it.

"Exactly," Claudia nodded. "It's a place that belongs to all of us, but in a very special way. It belongs to science. To wildlife. And to the future. No military. No mining, no cities. Just research stations, wild landscapes, and animals that can't be found anywhere else on Earth."

Dr. Harper added, "The treaty also protects this land from war and pollution. No weapons, no hunting. Everything we bring here? We take it back. Every scrap of trash, even food waste, goes back with us. Antarctica stays untouched."

Alexandra felt a strange kind of pride building in her chest. "So, it's a place where people actually work together to protect something? Like, really protect it?"

Claudia smiled. "That's right. It's one of the few places on Earth where international cooperation is working the way it should. Scientists from all over the world study this place together to understand our planet and how to protect it. But the treaty will need to undergo a review of all the consultative parties in 2048. That's why groups like the Antarctic Rights Alliance are pushing to make its protections stronger and permanent."

Alexandra looked back at the at the logo on Dr. Harper's mug. "So the Alliance wants to protect Antarctica like it has its own rights?"

"Exactly. They believe Antarctica deserves its own rights, like a voice," Claudia explained. "Not just because it's beautiful or important, but because the ice, the wildlife, and the ocean currents all matter on their own. It's about seeing nature not just as something we use, but something we're responsible for, as a living system we must respect."

Alexandra's notebook was already open on her lap. She wrote: *Treaty = promise. Alliance = voice for nature.*

Nestled in her bunk, Alexandra listened to the groan of ice against the hull as the ship rocked gently in the Antarctic night. She thought she saw the Ice Guardian's glowing figure in her dreams again, shimmering in the moonlight like a diamond on snow. The Guardian nodded approvingly, its presence calming and reassuring.

"You are the storyteller," the Guardian whispered, its voice like wind across a frozen plain. *"Your words can protect this place."*

MEETING THE PENGUINS

The ship anchored near a rocky island, its hull scraping gently against the icy water. Alexandra's heart raced as she prepared to ride to shore in a zodiac, an inflatable boat with a tough, rubberized bottom, perfect for navigating through the icy waters of Antarctica. The crew gathered their gear and climbed aboard, the motor starting with a roar as they zipped across the cold, choppy sea.

As the zodiac neared the shore, Alexandra could already hear the loud chorus of squawks and chirps. Then, she smelled it, a sharp, fishy scent carried on the wind. It was the unmistakable smell of penguins, and it hit Alexandra like a wave.

"Whoa," she coughed, waving a hand in front of her face. "It smells like a thousand fish had a food fight and lost."

Aunt Claudia chuckled. "That, my dear, is the unmistakable scent of guano. Penguin poop, nature's finest perfume."

Alexandra gagged dramatically. "And I thought my brother's gym socks were bad."

She leaned forward, her excitement building. Thousands of penguins were scattered across the rocky beach, their black-and-white feathers stark against the snow and rocks. They were much smaller than she imagined, and impossibly cute, like tiny tuxedoed clowns, waddling and sliding around without a care. Some even porpoised through the waves beside the zodiac, their sleek bodies arching gracefully out of the water before splashing back in.

The zodiac slowed as they approached, and Alexandra could hear the penguins' calls growing louder as she made her way to shore. The air was filled with the sounds of squawking penguins, their chicks chirping, and the rush of waves crashing on the shore. On land, Alexandra stood frozen, taking it all in—the noise, the energy, the sense of wonder. She was standing on the edge of a wild, unspoiled world where humans were definitely not in charge.

A group of Adélie penguins waddled across the ice, their short, stubby wings splayed back as they hopped over rocks. Alexandra giggled when one curious penguin waddled up and pecked at her boot, clearly unbothered by her presence.

Dr. Harper knelt beside her with a smile. "Adélies might seem clumsy on land, but in the water, they're like rockets. They can swim up to 15 km per hour, diving deep to hunt for food. Their powerful wings are shaped like flippers to help them glide through the water."

Alexandra watched as a parent penguin fed its chick, regurgitating a meal of krill into the chick's open beak. The sight of the fluffy chicks and their devoted parents made Alexandra's heart swell. She smiled, but then, as she imagined the challenges the penguins must face to provide for their young, her smile faded, and a thought tugged at her.

"Remember when we talked about krill?" Dr. Harper asked, her voice turning serious. "That's what penguins eat, but it's becoming harder for them to find enough. Climate change is pushing the sea ice to melt faster than usual. Because krill live in, on, and under the ice, if the ice melts too quickly, there won't be enough krill for the penguins to eat."

Alexandra nodded, remembering their earlier conversation. "So, they have to swim further to find food now, right?"

"Exactly," Dr. Harper said. "Penguins are being forced to swim further than they ever have before to find enough krill to feed themselves and their chicks. And that's a big problem, because they're using up more energy to get to their food."

A cold wind whipped across Alexandra's face, splashing her with tiny drops of rain as she looked up at the darkening sky. Above her, two small seabirds called Wilson's storm petrels zipped through the air, their dark wings fluttering as they swooped down to skim the water for food. Farther out, a much bigger bird called a giant petrel soared low over the waves, its huge wings helping it glide smoothly across the choppy sea.

Dr. Harper followed her gaze. "They're looking for krill, too," she said. "It's not just penguins. Seabirds like petrels and terns rely on krill as well, along with whales and even orcas. If their numbers drop, it ripples through the whole food web. If there's less krill, like we said before, it affects the whole food web!"

Alexandra watched as one of the petrels snatched something from the surface. She hadn't thought about the birds before, but it made sense.
"So if krill disappear, a lot of animals are in trouble," she murmured, jotting another note in her book.

Alexandra hesitated before asking, "And… isn't there another reason krill are disappearing? I overheard someone mention something about overfishing earlier."

Dr. Harper gave her an approving nod. "Yes, good memory. Overfishing means that too many krill are being taken out of the ocean before their population can bounce back. It's a big issue in the Southern Ocean, where most of the krill live. And here's the tricky part—people are catching krill for things like fish food, cosmetics, and even some health supplements. It's a little strange, right? You wouldn't think we'd be fishing for shrimp-sized creatures like that. But of course, this, too, makes life harder for all animals that rely on krill for food. The more krill we take, the less there is for these animals to eat."

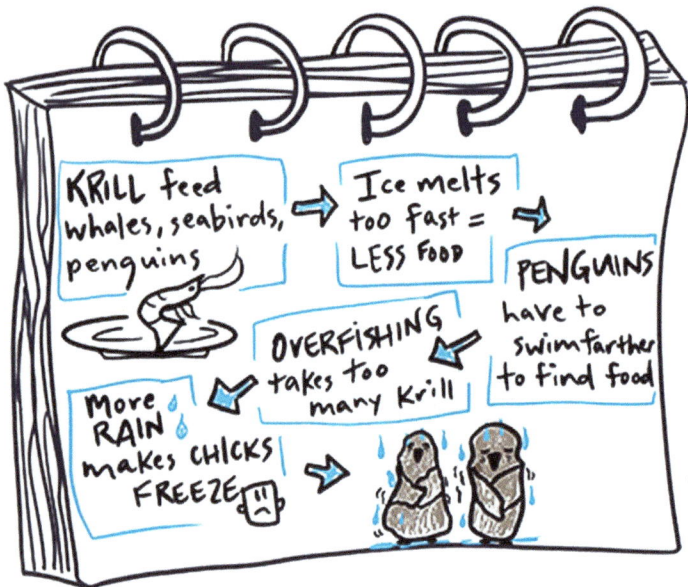

Alexandra quickly jotted down her thoughts in her notebook:

Krill feed whales, seabirds and penguins.

Ice melts too fast→less food.

Penguins have to swim farther to find food.

Overfishing takes too many krill.

A heavier gust of wind sent a fresh wave of icy drizzle across the landscape. Alexandra watched as the penguin chicks huddled closer to their parents, their soft down rustling in the wind. Some of them shook off water droplets, but others just stood there, shivering slightly.

Dr. Harper sighed. "And it's not just about food. We used to have about 25 to 80 days a year here where temperatures were above freezing. Soon, it'll be more like 35 to 130 days. That means more rain."

Alexandra frowned. "But why is rain so dangerous for the penguins?"

"Because Adélie chicks rely on their down to stay warm," Dr. Harper explained. "When it rains like this, their downy coats get soaked, and the cold winds can kill them. They can't survive when their down is wet." Alexandra swallowed hard, her fingers tightening around her pencil as she glanced back at the chicks. She added one more note to her list:

More rain → chicks can freeze.

The Ice Guardian's whisper returned, soft but clear: *"Even the smallest voices can make a difference."*

Alexandra stood still, surrounded by the bustling penguin colony, as the weight of Dr. Harper's words sank in. The reality of "just 1.5 degrees" of warming hit her hard. A small shift in temperature, and the difference between life and mass mortality for an entire generation of chicks became horribly real. This wasn't just something to read about—it was happening right in front of her. It was impossible to fully grasp the consequences of climate change, yet they were undeniable.

The Ice Guardian's voice echoed in her mind: *"The barriers you think exist are smaller than they seem. You already know what must be done. Will you act?"*

Alexandra's heart raced. The responsibility was enormous, but so was the potential to act. This wasn't just about penguins or rain—it was about the future of the Earth. About refusing to accept a future that wasn't worth fighting for.

The reminder of resilience wasn't just in nature; it was in every decision they made. She truly hoped even the smallest voices could make a difference.

Ghost Nets And Quiet Warnings

The zodiac rocked gently as Alexandra settled onto the side for the ride back to the ship, her boots braced against the rubber floor. The cold air pinched her cheeks, but her thoughts were still tangled with the day, of krill, penguins, and chicks huddling in the wind and rain.

Glancing back, she barely noticed the movement on shore at first. One of the guides, knee-deep in the icy shallows, was pulling something tangled and green from the water, but it wasn't seaweed. Alexandra watched as he wrestled with the mess, water droplets flinging into the air as he yanked and coiled the stringy mass, finally stuffing the bundle into his gear bag.

Beside her, the zodiac driver sighed. "Ghost net," he murmured. Alexandra turned to look at him. "What?"

"Lost fishing gear. Drifts for years, catching whatever swims into it." The driver's voice was calm, matter-of-fact. No anger, no alarm. Just… routine.

Looking back at the guide on shore, Alexandra saw he was already moving on, checking his pack, adjusting his gloves before hopping into the last zodiac. Like it was nothing. Like this kind of thing just happened.

Her stomach tightened as she glanced at the water, half-expecting to see more ghostly strands trailing beneath the surface. But the waves were smooth, erasing any sign that the net had ever been there.

How many things like that were out here?

What else drifted unseen, waiting?

The Ice Guardian's voice curled through her thoughts, quiet but certain: *"The things we ignore are often the things that need us most."*

She shivered, but not from the cold.

The zodiac driver revved the motor, turning them back toward the ship. The wind pressed against her, and Alexandra exhaled, watching her breath vanish into the gray sky. But the words from earlier, "Drifts for years, catching whatever swims into it.", echoed in her mind. The question of what happened to all the animals that got caught in those nets lingered, its weight settling deep inside her.

Later, as the ship swayed gently in the dark, Alexandra sat cross-legged on Aunt Claudia's bunk, pulling at the sleeves of her sweatshirt.
"I saw something today," she said.
Aunt Claudia looked up from her notebook, pushing her reading glasses onto her head. "Oh?"

"A ghost net," Alexandra whispered. "One of the guides pulled it in. It was just… floating out there."

Aunt Claudia's expression didn't change. No shock, no surprise. Just quiet understanding, the same reaction as the zodiac driver.

Alexandra frowned. "Wait. You already knew?"
Her aunt sighed, setting her notebook aside. "There's a lot we don't see, Alexandra. Even in places like this."

Alexandra swallowed. "What happens to the animals that get caught in them?"

Aunt Claudia didn't answer right away. She didn't have to. Alexandra could already picture it, the way a seal, a seabird, or even a whale might swim into the nearly invisible net, the frantic thrashing as it tried to escape, the slow, tightening grip when it couldn't. The weight dragging it down. The quiet, empty water after.

At last, her aunt spoke. "That's why we try to clean them up when we see them. And why so many people work to keep them out of the ocean in the first place. It's not just about saving the ones we see—it's about preventing harm before it happens."

She had spent the day learning about krill, about penguins, about how fragile even the strongest things could be. And now this—something else hidden in plain sight.

But noticing was the first step.

And once you see something, you can't unsee it.

Maybe that was where change began.

Ice Sculptor's Masterpiece

The next morning, Alexandra stretched and hopped in place on the deck, inhaling the crisp, Antarctic air deep into her lungs in the quiet dawn. Ahead, a massive iceberg cracked apart, unveiling stunning blue arches and twisting tunnels. Sunlight poured through, making the ice glow a deep, magical blue, like it was lit from within.

"It looks like a palace!" Alexandra gasped, hardly able to believe her eyes.

Dr. Harper grinned as she joined her. "In a way, it is. Icebergs are always changing, getting reshaped by the wind and waves. Some even have secret caves where seals go to hide from the storms. Like nature's own igloo."

Alexandra imagined seals sliding through icy hallways, penguins waddling down frosty corridors, and ice crystals sparkling like chandeliers. She pulled out her sketchbook, adding her own version of the magical palace.

As she stared, she noticed how the iceberg seemed almost alive, like it was stretching and yawning after a long night. The ice groaned and creaked, like an old giant waking up.

"Do you think the iceberg has a name?" Alexandra wondered aloud.

Dr. Harper chuckled. "If it did, I bet it would be something like 'The Grand Frosty' or 'Sir Cracks-a-lot.' These icebergs carry ice that's been around for thousands of years, but the iceberg itself is just a few months or a few years old. It's always shifting and changing."

Alexandra smiled. The iceberg felt like it was part of some ancient, forgotten kingdom, with stories to tell if you could only listen closely enough. She sketched faster, adding details of the giant ice columns and arches, imagining it as a frozen castle for seals, penguins, and maybe even a whale or two.

"But, like all castles," Dr. Harper said, her voice soft, "this one won't last forever. Icebergs break apart and melt back into the sea."

Alexandra frowned. "Is that normal?"

Dr. Harper nodded, but her smile faded, and her eyes grew serious. "Some melting is normal, ice moves and changes all the time. But right now, it's melting faster than it ever has before. Because of climate change, the planet is getting warmer, and the ice is disappearing quickly. This is a big problem. Penguins are losing their homes, whales are finding less food, and even the water we drink could be affected if the ice keeps melting."

Alexandra's pencil pressed harder into her notebook as she thought about ice disappearing. The Ice Guardian's whisper seemed to return, soft but clear: *"Nothing lasts forever. Protect what you can."*

Alexandra nodded to herself, feeling a quiet determination. She didn't know how yet, but she knew she'd protect whatever she could. She looked back at the iceberg, still glowing in the sun, and imagined it laughing like an old friend. "Hang in there, Sir Cracks-a-lot. I've got your back."

ICE IS NICE

As they kept sailing, Alexandra stared at the massive icebergs, still in awe of their jagged peaks, different shapes, and glowing blue crevices. Some were like frozen mountains, adrift in the sea. "It's hard to believe an iceberg just broke off something bigger," she said.

Dr. Harper nodded. "That's the thing about Antarctica. It's constantly changing." Pointing at one stunning iceberg, she said, "it probably calved, or broke off from an ice shelf, one of the floating tongues of ice that stretch from glaciers into the sea."

Alexandra frowned. "Wait, so it's not part of a glacier?"

"Not exactly," Dr. Harper said. "Glaciers are actually rivers of ice that flow downhill and they are on land. Some glaciers end on the land, but others are called marine-terminating glaciers because they reach the ocean and drop smaller icebergs straight into the water." She pointed toward the horizon. "But the real giants, like this one, come from something else called ice shelves."

"So, ice shelves are like… giant floating extensions of glaciers?" Alexandra asked.

"Exactly. They fill bays and inlets, growing over time until a huge chunk breaks off." Dr. Harper gestured toward the iceberg. "And that's how we get these massive icebergs."

Alexandra squinted, still amazed by the size of some floating ice that was flat, like a massive table. It looked big enough to hold a whole city. "That is massive! How big can these things get?"

Dr. Harper grinned. "You're looking at a perfect example, named the A80a iceberg. It's one of the biggest tabular icebergs to break off in recent years. It's about 1,500 square kilometers in size, that's bigger than the island of Bermuda, or 200,000 soccer fields!!"

Alexandra's eyes widened. "Wait, that's huge! Is it as tall as it is wide? I mean, is it like a giant chunk of ice floating upright? And what do you mean 'tabular iceberg'?"

Dr. Harper shook her head with a smile. "Great questions! A tabular iceberg like A80a, isn't really tall like a mountain. Instead, it's huge and flat—almost like a giant floating table of ice. The width of it stretches far across the ocean, but the height above the water is only about 30 to 50 meters. The majority of the iceberg, about 90%, is underwater."

Alexandra's brain was swirling trying to picture it. "So it's more like a floating ice sheet, not a big pointy iceberg? And that's why we can't really see where it begins and ends?"

"Exactly," Dr. Harper said. "A tabular iceberg has steep sides and a flat top, kind of like a giant slice of cake floating in the ocean."

Alexandra gazed out at the horizon, imagining the iceberg's hidden bulk beneath the surface. "That's wild." Then she asked, "But icebergs are already floating in the ocean, so if they melt, you said they don't make the sea levels rise, right?"

"Smart thinking," Dr. Harper smiled. "That's right—icebergs and sea ice don't raise sea levels when they melt because they're already displacing water, just like an ice cube melting in a glass of water. But glaciers are different. When glaciers melt or break off into the ocean, that's new water being added to the sea."

"And that's what makes sea levels rise?" Alexandra asked.

"Bingo."

Alexandra let out a slow breath, glancing at the endless ice around them. "There's so much I didn't know about ice."

Claudia grinned. "Oh, we haven't even gotten to the weirdest part yet. Ever heard of a brinicle?"

Alexandra shook her head.

Claudia wiggled her fingers. "Imagine an icicle… but upside-down, and growing underwater. Brinicles form when super-salty, freezing water sinks from sea ice. It's so cold that it freezes the seawater around it, creating a tube of ice that stretches down like a frozen finger of doom."

Alexandra's mouth dropped open. "That sounds terrifying."

"Oh, it is," Claudia said, her eyes twinkling. "Anything slow enough to get caught in one—like a sea star—freezes solid."

Alexandra shivered. "Okay, noted. Stay away from brinicles."

Dr. Harper smiled. "Antarctica's ice is full of surprises. But the most important thing to remember is that it's all connected. Ice shelves, glaciers, icebergs, sea ice—it all plays a role in keeping the planet in balance."

Alexandra gazed back at the tabular iceberg, its surface reflecting in the golden light. It wasn't just a frozen mountain. It was part of something bigger, something alive, moving, and changing.

Alexandra rubbed her forehead like she was trying to fit all the puzzle pieces together. "Okay, let me see if I've got this," she said. "Glaciers are big, slow rivers of ice. Some end on land, but the ones that reach the ocean are called marine-terminating glaciers, and they make little icebergs."

Dr. Harper nodded.

"But the really big icebergs come from ice shelves, which are already in the water—like floating extensions of glaciers," Alexandra continued. "And when those break off, they don't make sea levels rise because they've already displaced water, but when glaciers melt or lose ice into the ocean, that's when the water level rises."

"Yep," Dr. Harper said, smiling.

"And sea ice is just frozen ocean water," Alexandra said, recalling something she had read about it before. "It melts and refreezes every year, so it doesn't change sea levels either." She paused. "And then there are brinicles, which sound absolutely terrifying."

Claudia laughed. "Nailed it."

Alexandra let out a breath. "Okay. So icebergs, glaciers, sea ice, ice shelves, and brinicles. That's a lot of ice to keep track of." She looked toward a nearby glowing blue iceberg. "But I guess it's kind of important when you're in Antarctica."

Seals And Feathers

Alexandra's eyes widened as she stepped off the zodiac onto today's destination with a rocky shore, the gray skies overhead casting a soft, muted light over everything. There, nestled among the ice and pebbles, were several elephant seals, their oversized bodies flopping about as they molted. The ground was covered in a blizzard of molting fur, clumps of it floating like tumble weeds across the sand, catching the wind.

"Look at them!" Alexandra whispered, watching a few seals awkwardly wriggle and scratch at themselves as patches of old fur came off in big chunks. Their faces were like giant, wrinkled pillows, and their eyes blinked slowly as they lounged under the gray skies, belching and rolling over awkwardly, seemingly unbothered by the chaos around them.

"They're going through something called 'catastrophic molting,'" Dr. Harper explained, crouching beside Alexandra. "That's when animals lose almost all their fur or feathers at once, like a complete wardrobe change. It's a pretty intense process, but it helps them stay healthy by getting rid of old, worn-out fur."

As Alexandra watched, Gentoo penguins and a rogue Chinstrap penguin waddled by, their own molted feathers drifting in the air like confetti, their squawks filling the space. Some of the feathers, Alexandra noticed, were caught on the seals' rough hides, giving them an almost comical look, like they were wrapped in cozy blankets made of penguin feathers. The scene felt strangely peaceful, despite the ongoing molting madness.

"Those are fur seals over there," Dr. Harper said, pointing to a small group lounging on the dark sand. "They like to rest on the warmer patches of the beach, but they're not as big as the elephant seals and they're phenomenal divers. They're pretty fast, though, so if they decide to come after you, cross your arms in the air and shout at them! If that fails, hold your hand out and use the force!" , she said as she laughed.

As Alexandra took in the scene, she spotted two leopard seals lounging on the ice nearby, their long bodies stretched lazily across the frozen surface. They were massive, their sharp eyes scanning the landscape with a calm, watchful air. Though usually solitary, these seals didn't seem to mind sharing their ice today. Alexandra could imagine them slipping into the water, their long, sleek forms moving silently beneath the waves as they hunted.

But something was missing. Alexandra's gaze swept the horizon, yet she didn't see the crabeater seals, the ones who were supposed to thrive here, feeding on krill in the frigid waters.

"Where are the crabeaters?" Alexandra asked.

Dr. Harper's voice softened. "They've been harder to find in recent years. Crabeater seals rely on krill, but as the ocean's temperature shifts, those tiny, crucial creatures are becoming more scarce in some areas. It's just one of many changes we're seeing, and we don't yet know what it means for the entire ecosystem."

Alexandra nodded, scanning the ice for any sign of movement. A flicker of uncertainty settled in her chest, but Dr. Harper wasn't finished.

"Some of our colleagues, other guides, have reported large numbers of crabeater seals farther south this week, about 150 miles from here," Dr. Harper continued. "That suggests they might be following the krill to cooler waters. But whether this is a temporary change or part of a bigger pattern, we still don't know."

Alexandra glanced at Dr. Harper, realizing how many people were paying attention—each sighting, each report, another piece of a puzzle no one had fully solved.

"That's the thing about Antarctica," Dr. Harper said. "It's changing in ways we don't always understand. Scientists are constantly working to make sense of it, but the picture comes together from many sources including guides, researchers, even casual observers who notice something different. Sometimes, the smallest details turn out to be the most important."

Alexandra looked out at the seals, the penguins, and the dark, rolling waters beyond. The scene felt quieter than usual, and she could almost hear the land holding its breath. The lack of crabeaters was a small sign, but it was a sign of something bigger, a world changing in ways that were harder to see, yet impossible to ignore. The sight of these animals molting, lounging, and resting, each species in its own rhythm, was a powerful reminder of how even the most resilient creatures couldn't escape the forces of change. In the midst of it all, the seals were still here, still hanging on. It gave Alexandra hope that, perhaps, they weren't too late to make a difference.

As she sketched in her notebook, Alexandra felt the faintest whisper—a shift in the wind, or maybe something else. A reminder. Change was everywhere, in the missing seals, in the shifting ice, even in the patterns of krill beneath the surface. But noticing the smallest details meant they weren't lost. She closed her eyes for a moment. *"Things are changing,"* the whisper seemed to say. "But the ice, the animals, the food web, they're still here," she whispered back, the words a protective promise.

Antarctica's Toughest Garden

"True or false," Dr. Harper began, her voice carrying over the crunch of snow beneath their boots. "Antarctica has no plants at all."

Alexandra grinned. "False! I know there are plants here! I've read about them."

"Very good," Dr. Harper said with a smile. "But did you know that the only flowering plants in Antarctica, the southernmost flowering plants on the planet, are smaller than your hand?"

Alexandra's eyes widened. "Really? What are they?"

Dr. Harper knelt down and pointed to a cluster of green tufts peeking out from between the rocks. "Meet Antarctic hair grass and Antarctic pearlwort, the only two flowering plants tough enough to survive here."

Alexandra crouched beside her, examining the tiny plants. The hair grass looked like miniature clumps of grass, while the pearlwort formed small, cushion-like patches with delicate yellow flowers.

"They're so small!" Alexandra exclaimed.

"Exactly," Dr. Harper said. "Staying small and low to the ground helps them avoid Antarctica's brutal winds. But that's not their only trick." She began ticking off adaptations on her fingers:

- Super-strong roots anchor them in the thin Antarctic soil, where nutrients are scarce.
- They can survive being frozen solid during the long Antarctic winters.
- Without insects to pollinate them, they rely on wind pollination and can also self-pollinate to reproduce.

Alexandra leaned closer, her breath fogging in the icy air. "They're like little superheroes!"

Dr. Harper chuckled. "They really are! And here's something even more fascinating: while these flowering plants are spreading because of warming temperatures, they're competing with other hardy survivors like mosses and lichens."

Alexandra looked around, noticing patches of emerald green moss clinging to the rocks nearby. "What makes them so special?"

"Mosses and lichens are some of the first life forms to colonize Antarctica," Dr. Harper explained. "Lichens are special because they're made up of both fungi and algae, and they're tough enough to survive here. They help hold the soil together and add nutrients that other plants need. In such a harsh place, every living thing plays an important role!"

Alexandra nodded, imagining yet another bustling world hidden beneath the snow and nestled in the rock crevasses.

"So they're all part of a bigger picture."

"Exactly." Dr. Harper said, her eyes sparkling with enthusiasm. "As Antarctica warms due to climate change, it's crucial to study how these different species interact and adapt."

As she looked at the tiny green patches dotting the otherwise barren landscape, Alexandra asked, "Is that... good or bad?"

Dr. Harper sighed thoughtfully. "It's complicated. On one hand, it shows how resilient life can be, even in a place as remote and unforgiving as this. But on the other hand, it's a sign that Antarctica is changing rapidly because of our planet getting steadily warmer."

As Alexandra stood up, she noticed something glinting in the distance, a faint shimmer on the horizon where ice met sky. It was almost imperceptible, but she felt a strange sense of calm wash over her.

"Dr. Harper," Alexandra said softly, still staring at the horizon, "do you think... the Ice Guardian is watching us?"

Dr. Harper followed her gaze and smiled knowingly. "Some say the Ice Guardian is always watching, protecting this fragile world." She paused before adding, "But perhaps it's also reminding us that we have a part to play in protecting it, too."

Alexandra nodded solemnly, feeling an increasing sense of responsibility settle over her, like standing tall in the face of a fierce storm. Despite the cold, she felt determined to take on the challenge.

As they continued their trek across the rocky and icy terrain, Alexandra couldn't help but glance back at the tiny plants clinging to life against all odds. Though small and soft, they were a testament to the resilience and strength of Antarctica itself, and to the ways every part of this land, no matter how seemingly insignificant, played a role in the planet's delicate balance. She vowed to do her part to protect them.

Ghosts of Whalers Bay

The ship slipped through Neptune's Bellows, the jagged rock walls towering on either side like the mouth of some ancient sea creature. Alexandra shivered, though the air wasn't particularly cold. It was the stillness—the way the mist curled low over the black water, swallowing sound, muffling even the ship's engine.

They weren't sailing into just any harbor. They were entering the flooded heart of a volcano.

"Welcome to Deception Island," Aunt Claudia said, her voice quiet but certain. "This is a caldera, a collapsed volcanic crater. The water beneath us used to be solid ground until the whole thing caved in. And the island? It's still alive."

Alexandra's stomach dropped as she peered over the side. The idea of floating over a sunken volcano—one that could still erupt—sent a prickle up her spine.

Minutes later, she climbed into the zodiac, clutching the side as they sped toward shore. The beach was black volcanic sand, steaming in places as if the Earth were whispering its secrets. Small bubbles popped at the water's edge, fizzing like invisible breath.

As Alexandra stepped onto land, she glanced up the dark slopes surrounding them. No towering ice cliffs here. The caldera walls were bare, dusted with patches of moss, not snow.

"There used to be more ice here," Claudia said quietly.

Alexandra swallowed hard.

Ahead, the ruins of Whalers Bay loomed through the mist and gray skies—massive rusted tanks, skeletal wooden buildings, wooden boats, and the ghosts of an industry that had once seen itself as heroic, before the world realized the cost.

"Between 1911 and 1931, they processed between 4,000 and 8,000 whales right here. Right where you're standing," Claudia said, her voice barely louder than the wind.

Incredulous, she tried to wrap her mind around the number. She thought back to the humpback whale she'd seen days ago, its sleek body cutting through the waves, the way it had seemed to watch her just as much as she had watched it. "But weren't they already rare back then?"

Claudia nodded. "Some species, yes. Others, not yet. But whalers didn't really think about things like sustainability. There was always another whale just beyond the horizon." She gestured toward the water. "At least, that's what they believed."

"This was one of the busiest whaling stations in Antarctica. At its peak, the factory ships and land-based stations here could strip down a whale in less than thirty minutes. Every single part was processed including blubber, meat and bones."

Alexandra gasped. "I thought they only wanted the oil."

"They did, at first," Claudia said. "In the early days, whalers only used the blubber because whale oil was in high demand for lamps, soaps, and even explosives. But as whaling changed, so did the way they used the whales. By the 1930s, huge factory ships took over. Instead of bringing whales to land, they processed everything right on the ship, the meat for food, the bones for fertilizer, baleen for umbrellas and corsets, and even the blood for industrial products. That meant almost nothing went to waste."

Alexandra peered through the misty rain along the steaming black volcanic beach, suddenly aware of how quiet it was. She tried to imagine it as it had been a century ago–nothing like this peaceful, albeit eerie, scene. She could almost hear the clang of metal, the hiss of steam rising from massive vats, the heavy thud of whale carcasses dragged ashore. The air would have been thick with the choking stench of blubber being boiled down, the shouts of men working through the endless procession of giants from the sea. Back then, they believed they were fueling progress, providing oil to light homes and power industries.

A gust of wind whipped down the bay, rattling the skeletal remains of the old wooden station. Claudia adjusted her hood and turned back toward the group, but Alexandra lingered, feeling the weight of history pressing against her.

That night, safe on the ship as they drifted in the caldera's unsettling stillness, Alexandra was still thinking about Whalers Bay when one of the naturalists slid into a chair beside her.

"Ever hear the story of the Ghost Whales?" she asked, her voice dropping to a conspiratorial whisper.

Alexandra's eyebrows furrowed. "Ghost Whales?"

The naturalist's face took on a serious tone. "Some say, if you stand on the shore at night, you can still hear them. The whales that were slaughtered here, calling out, their voices still trapped in the mist. Warning the living to remember them."

A gust of wind rattled the windows, and the old ship groaned in response. Alexandra shivered but forced a laugh. "It's just the wind."

Claudia raised her mug, her eyes glinting. "Or is it?"

Later, as Alexandra lay in her bunk, the ship rocking gently beneath her, she heard it. A deep, mournful sound, echoing over the waves. A long, low moan.

She sat up, her heart pounding. The sound came again, distant but unmistakable.

A whale song.

She scrambled to the porthole, pressing her forehead to the cold glass. Outside, the ocean stretched into endless blackness, the silhouette of Whalers Bay barely visible under the pale moonlight.

She listened, barely breathing.

Not ghosts.

She thought she had come to observe. But now, she knew—she was part of the story.

GUARDIANS OF THE PLANET

Alexandra leaned against her favorite spot on the railing, staring out at the icy water. Deception Island still haunted her. The rusting vats, the wind howling through empty buildings, the crosses on stone piles to mark the lives of long-ago workers. Even the ghosts of whales seemed to linger there. But here, in the open sea, the world felt alive.

Claudia walked up beside her, holding a tablet in one hand and something wrapped in a napkin in the other. "Fresh data straight from the researchers at Palmer Station," she announced, grinning. "And, in true Palmer tradition, a freshly baked chocolate brownie."

Alexandra raised an eyebrow. "Are these things connected?"
Claudia unwrapped the gooey square and handed it over. "You tell me. Some of the most valuable science—and the best brownies—come from Palmer Station, the smallest Antarctic Research Station, known for its marine and biological studies. Plus, it's the only one on the Antarctic Peninsula. We had planned to stop there, but there is too much ice to dock safely. We'll have to settle for their data."

Alexandra took a bite as Claudia tapped the screen. An image of krill, those tiny, shrimp-like creatures, popped up. "You know these guys, right? You know whales love them."

Alexandra nodded. "A whole lot of them make a whale-sized meal."

"Exactly. But check this out." Claudia swiped to another image. "This is a satellite image of phytoplankton, which are microscopic plants that float in the water. They soak up sunlight, absorb carbon dioxide, and produce oxygen, kind of like the ocean's version of a rainforest. In fact, scientists say phytoplankton produce over half of the oxygen on Earth."

"What's really cool is that these tiny ocean plants have chlorophyll just like leaves on trees, and satellites can spot that green glow from way up in space which is how we got this image."

Alexandra tilted her head, piecing it together. "So, phytoplankton use sunlight to grow, we use the oxygen, and krill eat the phytoplankton. Then, whales and other animals like penguins and seals eat the krill. It's all connected, right?"

Claudia's eyes sparkled. "Almost. But whales actually help the phytoplankton, too."

Alexandra frowned. "How?"

Claudia tapped again, pulling up a different satellite image.

"See this? Scientists track how nutrients move through the ocean.

When whales dive deep, they stir up iron and nitrogen from below. And when they—" she paused dramatically—"poop, they release even more nutrients right where phytoplankton need them."

Alexandra nearly choked on her brownie. "Did you just say whale poop feeds the ocean?"

Claudia grinned. "Yep! Whale poop is packed with iron, which is like fertilizer for phytoplankton. More iron means more phytoplankton, which means more food for krill, and more carbon pulled out of the atmosphere."

Alexandra's eyes widened. "So… more whales mean more phytoplankton. More phytoplankton mean less carbon dioxide in the air. And more oxygen for us?"

"Bingo. Plus, when whales die, their bodies sink, locking away even more carbon in the deep ocean. It's called a 'whale fall.' One whale can store more carbon than a forest of big oak trees over its lifetime."

Alexandra looked out at the water, her mind spinning. Yesterday, at Deception Island, whales had been nothing more than barrels of oil to the whalers. But now? Now she saw them for what they really were.

Essential to Earth's survival.

A shadow moved in the waves. Then another.

Alexandra held her breath as a burst of white spray shot into the air. A whale. Then another. A massive tail lifted, then disappeared into the deep.

Claudia nudged her. "See? They're out here, saving the planet."

Alexandra grinned and popped the last piece of brownie into her mouth. "Fertilize away, big guys. Fertilize away."

THE PROMISE

The ship's engines hummed as they slowly turned to head north and back home. Alexandra had been wrapped in a blanket on deck, gazing at the last shimmering glacier she might ever see as it slowly faded into the distance. The icy world she'd gotten to know so well was starting to slip away, and her heart felt heavy. It was hard to believe the adventure was coming to an end.

The crew had gathered in the research lab for one last meeting before they left the Antarctic Peninsula behind to discuss their findings and next steps. Alexandra joined them, sitting on a stool, gripping the notes and sketches she'd made during the trip.

"How do we help Antarctica?" Alexandra asked, looking up at Aunt Claudia.

She smiled and handed her a fresh notepad. "We tell people about it."

Alexandra flipped open the pad and began writing, "I'll start with the things I can do—sharing what I've learned with my classmates and being more mindful of the world around me."

Dr. Harper smiled gently. "Every little change counts—like turning off lights when you're not using them or picking up trash when you see it. And when lots of people do those things, it adds up! But we also need big changes. We need our leaders to make better choices too, like using clean energy and protecting places like Antarctica."

Aunt Claudia added, "That's why the Antarctic Treaty is so important, the agreement that countries from all over the world signed to make sure Antarctica is used for peace, science, and conservation. No one country can just take what they want from it. Instead, everyone works together to protect it."

Alexandra thought about how people from so many different places had agreed to care for one part of the world. She jotted it down in her notebook:

Big changes happen when people work together.

"The more we share what we've learned and speak up, the more we can help make those big changes happen," Dr. Harper said.

Alexandra nodded, feeling the weight of the responsibility that came with this new knowledge. She admired how so many countries in the world had signed the Antarctic Treaty to protect the continent, how nations were working together for something bigger than themselves.

"Change starts with one voice," Aunt Claudia said, her tone steady but hopeful.

Alexandra smiled. She already knew where she would start.

In the back of her mind, the Ice Guardian's presence lingered, no longer just a memory, but something alive in the wind, the waves, and even the ship's quiet creak as it sailed north. Alexandra felt it deep in her chest, steady and insistent. It wasn't just a reminder. It was a call. A promise. A challenge. A responsibility.

But she wasn't alone. Others had heard it too: Claudia, Dr. Harper, and the other scientists, the nations who signed the Antarctic Treaty, the Antarctic Rights Alliance, and more. Now she understood: her voice and choices were part of something much bigger. A movement already in motion, and one she was ready to help carry forward.

She closed her notebook and looked out over the sea, the horizon glowing with early light. Soon she'd be back in her classroom, among her classmates and friends.

And when she stood before them, she wouldn't just tell them what she saw. She'd ask them what they could do.

Because the whisper was still there.

And maybe, just maybe, they'd hear it, too.

The Return To School

The sounds were different now. No wind, no creaking ship, no crackling ice. Just the faint hum of fluorescent lights and the shuffle of sneakers on tile.

Alexandra stood at the front of her classroom, a large globe beside her and sunlight streaming through the windows—no longer across a frozen sea, but warming the room all the same. Her heart thudded with anticipation. This wasn't just about what she had seen. It was about passing it on, about turning wonder and curiosity into questions, and questions into action.

"This is how we usually see the world," Alexandra said, pointing to a normal map and parts of the globe. "But what if we looked at it like this?"

She reoriented the globe. Now, Antarctica was at the center, with all the continents surrounding it. Her classmates leaned in, intrigued by the fresh perspective.

"This is Antarctica," Alexandra continued, her voice steady but full of wonder. "It's not just at the bottom of the world. It's connected to all of us. Everything that happens there—whether it's the ice breaking, the whales pooping, or the penguins searching for krill—affects the whole planet."

She traced her fingers along the Southern Ocean. "The Southern Ocean controls weather everywhere. If Antarctica changes, it ripples out. It impacts everything."

Her classmates sat quietly, absorbing what she said. Antarctica wasn't just some cold, distant place anymore. It was part of the big picture. It was part of *them and their lives.*

Alexandra took a breath. "Before we left Antarctica, I talked to our ship's Ice Captain. She's the one who reads the ice, who figures out how to get the ship safely through when the path ahead isn't clear."

She glanced around the room. "I asked her how she knew where to go. She told me that no one ever has all the answers right away. The ice shifts. The conditions change. But you don't stop. You watch, you listen, and you keep moving forward, one decision at a time, using the best information you have at the time."

Alexandra let the words settle. "That's what I'm doing now. I don't have all the answers. None of us do. But I can start. I can share what I learned. I can listen. I can pay attention to what's happening, just like an Ice Captain reading the sea. We all share the same air, land, and water. And that's something worth protecting. "

She looked at the map one more time. "And maybe, together, we can find the best way forward."

For a moment, the classroom was quiet. Then, one of her friends raised a hand.

"How do we start?"

Alexandra smiled.

The Ice Guardian's presence was still there, steady as ever.

Not a promise. Not a burden. But a challenge.

To keep going. To keep wondering.

To keep navigating, even when the way forward wasn't clear.

She didn't have to do it alone.

And that, she realized, was the most important thing of all.

From Left to Right: Humpback whale so close we could count barnacles; iceberg palace; charismatic Weddell seal (aka, "George"); size of icebergs near ship as viewed from the zodiac; elephant seal molting amid the feathers of the molting penguins.

From Left to Right: Gentoo penguin with downy feathers; Chinstrap penguins on Half Moon Island in the snow and rain; a dramatic Antarctic horizon; Iceberg Alley; colony of Adelie penguins.

From Left to Right: Adelie penguin regurgitating food to its young; Neko Harbor; Deception Island and the oil vats; steaming shores within the Deception Island Caldera; remnants of whaling boats in Whalers Bay.

From Left to Right: A stunning iceberg that was a crowd favorite; Mariana and I pre-voyage in Ushuaia; boarding a zodiac; savoring some ancient ice; humpback whale breaching in the early morning hours--it literally brought me to tears.

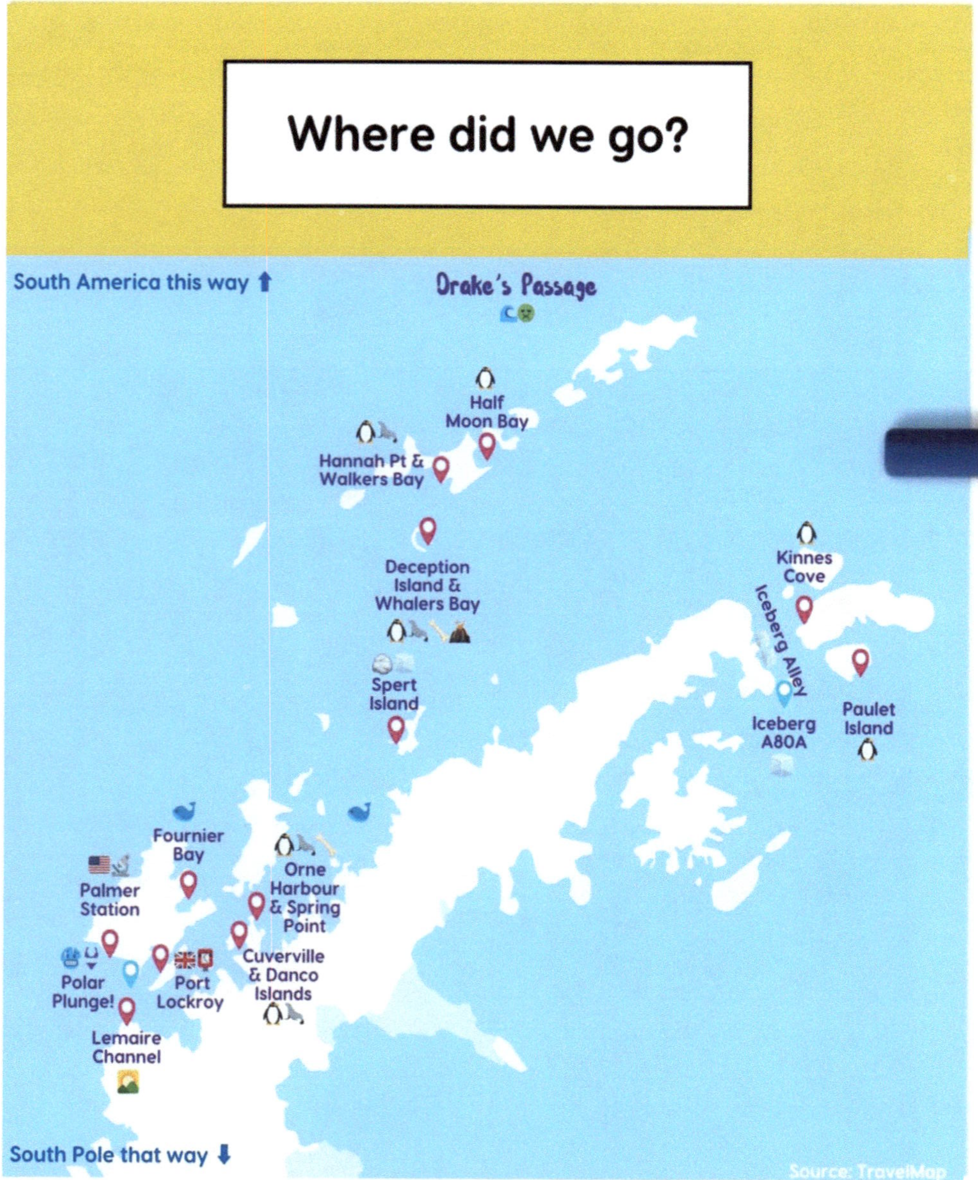

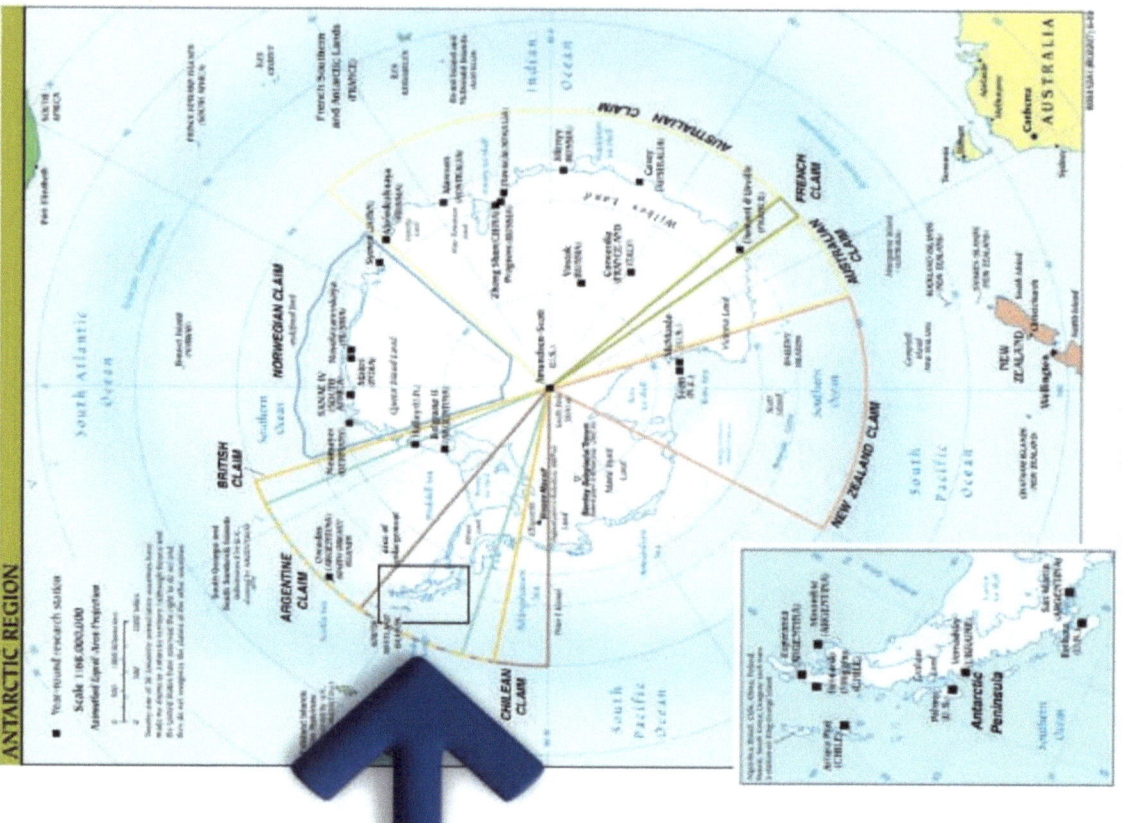

Where did we go?

This voyage map was created by Zoe Eather, science communicator and thinker extraordinaire. Note that we remained in the area of the Antarctic Peninsula throughout our journey.

https://commons.wikimedia.org/wiki/Category:Political_maps_of_Antarctica#/media/File:%22Antarctic_region%22_CIA_World_Factbook.jpg

My Antarctic Inspiration Squad: 124 women and gender-diverse leaders with STEMM backgrounds, changemakers each and every one, from over 20 different countries. Thank you.

ACKNOWLEDGMENTS

No one explores alone.

To the real-life ice guardians:

Thank you for holding the line between wonder and warning. Your wisdom, questions, and courage helped this story find its way through surreal landscapes, snowy zodiac rides, and icy mornings.

To the readers and adventurers, young and old:

You remind me daily that curiosity is a superpower.

To the scientists who study the sea, the ice, the sky, and all that live here:

Thank you for listening to the quiet hum of the planet, then speaking up so others might hear it, too.

To my Homeward Bound Antarctic Inspiration Squad:

You were my compass in the cold. With every message, memory, and moment of shared purpose, you helped shape this story's heart and helped me remember my own.

And finally, to Antarctica:

For showing us what stillness, strength, and surprising joy look like in icy form. May we always pay attention.

Special thanks to the Island Sky crew and staff, plus the naturalists who informed our journey with panache, and helped me fill my notebook on the daily: Iggy Rojas, Cat Totty, Fran Housdon, Linda Steutel, Scott Thompson, Rose Papworth, Marta Zetterstrom, Lisa Barry, Andy Schofield, and Carl Elkington. Any mistakes in this story are on me.

Extra thanks to the following for helping me launch this story: the real life Claudia Roedel, our Expedition Leader; Mark Brandon for his extra eyes on the science; and fellow HB thought leaders who helped me flesh out the story: Nad Kattan, Bridget Myers, Sarah Frankland, Gisele Montano, Jane Usher, and Nuwanthika Fernando.

Lastly, this story voyage was proudly approved by Junior Ice Captains Abdulkareem Alaska and Mariam Toonsi, whose curiosity thrived and questions charted bold paths...and not a single penguin filed a complaint.

About the Author

Wendi Pillars is a mom, a teacher, and a curious human who believes that wonder is one of our greatest superpowers. She traveled to Antarctica with Homeward Bound, a global leadership expedition made up of 124 incredible women and non-binary scientists, explorers, and changemakers. While sailing past icebergs and spotting penguins, Wendi filled her notebook with sketches, facts, and dreams, many of which became the pages of this story. When she's not writing or teaching, Wendi can often be found marveling at native bees, wandering through forests, or helping kids discover just how powerful their voices can be. This book is her love letter to the ice, the wild, and to every young storyteller who's ready to listen and protect what matters.

ABOUT THE ILLUSTRATOR

Hi, **I'm Mehar**, a children's book illustrator from Pakistan 🇵🇰 "A land cradled by snowy crowns and the timeless grace of majestic mountain ranges".

I bring stories to life with soft, whimsical watercolor art that's filled with warmth, imagination, and heart. With a background in Visual Communication Design, I've illustrated stories that celebrate wonder, kindness, and creativity.

When I'm not working, you'll usually find me traveling, exploring new cultures, or enjoying a cozy café with a croissant in hand. My greatest joy is creating illustrations that make children smile and turn each page into a little adventure of its own.

Polar Literacy Principles

The Polar Literacy Principles were developed through the Polar Literacy Initiative, a collaborative effort to support educators in teaching polar science. These seven principles provide a clear and accessible framework for understanding the importance of the Arctic and Antarctic to Earth's systems, and to us all.

Raising awareness of the polar regions has never been more urgent. These distant, frozen places may seem far removed from our daily lives, but they are central to Earth's climate, biodiversity, and ocean circulation. As the impacts of climate change accelerate, understanding the role of polar systems becomes critical for preparing the next generation of scientists, environmental stewards, and informed citizens.

In *Echoes of the Ice*, Alexandra's journey aligns closely with each of these principles, bringing the science, wonder, and fragility of Antarctica to life through story.

Learn more about the Polar Literacy Principles at:
polar-ice.org/polar-literacy-initiative

The Seven Polar Literacy Principles and How They Connect to the Story

1. The Arctic and Antarctic Regions are unique because of their location on Earth.

Alexandra witnesses the extremes of Antarctica's remoteness, including midnight sun, icy winds, and steaming volcanic sands on Deception Island. These dramatic features are shaped by Antarctica's location at the southernmost point on Earth, where latitude, unique ocean currents, isolation, and seasonal light cycles create one of the planet's most challenging environments.

2. Ice is the dominant feature of the Polar Regions.

Alexandra encounters glowing blue icebergs in Iceberg Alley, towering glacier walls, and sea ice that cracks and groans beneath her ship. She learns how Antarctic ice shapes everything from ocean salinity and currents to animal behavior and climate records locked deep within the ice itself.

3. Polar Regions play a central role in regulating Earth's weather and climate.

Through awe-filled conversations on deck, Alexandra learns about the Southern Ocean's global "conveyor belt", a current formed when cold, salty water sinks to the ocean floor and flows around the planet. She also crosses the Antarctic Convergence, a boundary where cold polar water collides with warmer ocean water, creating powerful mixing zones that influence weather patterns and carbon cycling worldwide.

4. The Polar Regions have productive food webs.

Alexandra marvels at how tiny krill support an entire ecosystem, feeding whales, penguins, seals, and seabirds. She learns about bioluminescent phytoplankton and how these microscopic plant-like organisms form the base of the polar food chain, absorbing carbon dioxide and producing oxygen. Every creature is connected, from the tiniest glow to the breach of a humpback whale.

5. The Poles are experiencing the effects of climate change at an accelerating rate.

As Alexandra observes melting ice, nesting penguins coping with rain and warm temperatures, and shifting krill populations, she begins to understand the rapid transformations happening in Antarctica. The story shows how changes in sea ice and temperature affect everything from ecosystems and ocean currents to animal migrations.

6. Humans are a part of the Polar system. The Arctic has a rich cultural history and diversity of Indigenous Peoples.

While the Antarctic has no permanent residents or Indigenous populations, Alexandra explores how human influence still shapes the region through international cooperation, research, and environmental protection. She learns about the Antarctic Treaty, the Antarctic Rights Alliance, and the responsibility humans have in preserving a place that belongs to all.

7. New technologies, sensors and tools — as well as new applications of existing technologies — are expanding scientists' abilities to study the land, ice, ocean, atmosphere and living creatures of the Polar Regions.

From digital mapping and remotely operated underwater vehicles to net trawls and satellite data, Alexandra joins researchers using modern tools to study krill, measure ocean temperature, and learn about ice melt. Her own storytelling becomes a form of citizen science amplifying what she learns for others.

In every icy breath and glowing iceberg, Alexandra's story helps young readers build their own sense of polar literacy and a desire to protect what they now understand.

TEACHER RESOURCES: VOCABULARY & DISCUSSION/ REFLECTION QUESTIONS

Vocabulary List: (adjust for your students in your specific context)

Tier 1 (Basic Vocabulary): ice, whale, penguin, ocean, sea, seal, ship

Tier 2 (High-Frequency Vocabulary): expedition, ecosystem, adventure, climate, habitat, encounter, guardian, nutrients, garden, bustling, ripples, frigid, lingered, groan, eerie

Tier 3 (Domain-Specific Vocabulary): krill, calving, Antarctic Treaty, phytoplankton, glacier, ice shelf, iceberg, spyhopping, fluttered, jagged, parka, fluke, salps, porpoised, regurgitating, moulted/molted, Drake Passage, Ushuaia, and other specific place names.

Pre-assessment Questions:

These questions can help teachers gauge students' prior knowledge about polar environments, ecosystems, and related scientific concepts. Again, they are suggestions. Use them as a launch point and adjust for your students in your context.

Multiple Choice Questions (Circle the best answer):

1. **Which continent is the coldest and driest on Earth?**
    A) Asia.
    B) Antarctica.
    C) North America.
    D) Europe.

2. **What is unique about the Southern Ocean?**
    A) It is the smallest ocean.
    B) It is completely covered in ice all year.
    C) It connects all the world's oceans with powerful currents.
    D) It has no marine life.

3. **What is "calving" in Antarctica?**
    A) When seals give birth.
    B) When a chunk of glacier ice breaks off into the sea.
    C) When penguins molt.
    D) When snow falls heavily.

4. **Why does ancient Antarctic ice appear blue?**
    A) It's dyed by algae.
    B) It reflects the ocean.
    C) It's frozen saltwater.
    D) It's so dense that only blue light escapes.

5. **What role do krill play in the Southern Ocean ecosystem?**
    A) They are apex predators.
    B) They provide food for whales, seals, and penguins.
    C) They produce icebergs.
    D) They have no ecological importance.

True or False Questions:

1. Antarctica is the only continent with no permanent human residents. (T)
2. The Antarctic Treaty was created to protect Antarctica for science and peace. (T)
3. Melting sea ice directly raises global sea levels. (F; melting glaciers do)
4. Whale poop helps fertilize phytoplankton, which supports ocean food webs. (T)
5. Krill populations are unaffected by changes in sea ice. (F; they rely on sea ice)

Open-Ended Questions:

1. What do you already know about the Antarctic ecosystem and the types of animals that live there? (living organisms, climate, unique features, location, etc.)
2. Why do you think it is important to study polar environments like Antarctica? What impacts could changes in these regions have on the planet?
3. Describe one way that human activities might affect life in polar regions.

Critical Thinking Questions for the story as a whole: Use these questions before, during, or after reading Echoes from the Ice to encourage curiosity, critical thinking, and classroom conversation. Questions range from surface-level recall to deeper analysis and personal reflection.

DOK 1: Recall & Comprehension
- Where does Alexandra travel?
- What kind of weather does Alexandra experience in Antarctica?
- Name one animal Alexandra encounters on her journey.
- What is climate change, in your own words?
- What do scientists study in Antarctica?

DOK 2: Skills & Concepts
- Why is Antarctica important for studying Earth's climate?
- Compare your home to Antarctica. How are they different?
- How are they similar?
- How does Alexandra show curiosity during her journey?
- What are some clues that show how the climate is changing?
- How does the melting of glaciers affect the ocean and marine life?

DOK 3: Strategic Thinking
- Why do you think Alexandra chose to listen to the ice? What does that mean?
- How does the setting affect Alexandra's understanding of the planet?
- What role does observation play in both science and storytelling in this book?
- How might Alexandra's experience inspire other young people?
- Discuss the impact of overfishing on the krill population and what that means for the food web in Antarctica.

DOK 4: Extended Thinking
- Imagine you could ask Antarctica a question—what would it be? What might its answer be?
- Design a short action project for your community inspired by Alexandra's story.
- Write a letter from the perspective of a glacier, explaining what you've seen change over time.
- Create a visual metaphor for what the "whispers of the ice" represent.
- If you were in charge of protecting Antarctica, what specific actions would you take to ensure its preservation for future generations?

Extension Ideas
- **Mapping Prompt:** Trace a path from your home to Antarctica on a map. Label the Drake Passage, Deception Island, Palmer Station.
- **Vocabulary Challenge:** Identify and define science-related words in the story (e.g., glacier, ecosystem, climate, data).
- **Science Connection:** Research one way scientists study ice in Antarctica. Share what tools or methods they use.

Deeper Thinking Prompts:

1. Why do you think the Antarctic Treaty is important for the future of Earth?
2. Alexandra realized "small things make a big difference." What does that mean in the story? What about in real life?

Creative Story Sparks:

1. Create your own nature guardian for a place you love. What do they protect? What do they whisper?
2. Imagine a journal entry Alexandra writes after she returns home—what does she still wonder about?

Map + Place Exploration Prompts:

(Encourage readers to become mini cartographers!)

- Find:
    - The Drake Passage
    - Deception Island and Whalers Bay
    - The Antarctic Peninsula
    - The Southern Ocean

- Challenge activity: Have students draw a "circular world map" with Antarctica at the center. How does that change how they think about the planet?

Mini STEM Research Sparks:

Encourage readers to choose their own investigation topics:

- How do scientists track whales?
- What is bioluminescence and why do deep-sea creatures glow?
- Why is sea ice so important for the planet?
- What makes volcanoes under ice unique?

What questions can your students come up with out of curiosity?

Do Something: Real-World Action Prompts

To connect to the story's theme and give kids a voice:

- Write a letter to someone in your town about why Antarctica matters.
- Make a mini-poster to teach your classmates one new thing about Antarctica.
- Reduce single-use plastic for a week and track your impact.
- Create a class "Plan A" for protecting something local.

Additional resources for further study about Polar regions:

Here are some suggested resources (for starters!) for further reading on polar literacy, polar science, and related educational materials:

1. **Polar Educators International (PEI):**
   - The PEI website offers a wealth of resources, including the Polar Literacy Principles, lesson plans, and teaching materials designed to engage students in learning about polar regions.
   - Website: Polar Educators International https://polareducator.org/

2. **National Snow and Ice Data Center (NSIDC):**
   - NSIDC provides educational resources, data, and research related to snow and ice, including extensive information on Arctic and Antarctic environments.
   - Website: NSIDC Education Resources
     https://nsidc.org/learn/what-cryosphere

3. **The Arctic Council:**
   - The Arctic Council's website includes reports and resources related to Arctic governance, climate change, and indigenous knowledge, offering insights into the socio-political aspects of polar regions.
   - Website: Arctic Council https://arctic-council.org/

4. **Cosmos Education:**
   - Learning resources and teacher tools linked to the Australian National Curriculum to inspire and support STEM teaching. Access collections to explore the latest content, or review by subject, topic, year level and type. Includes videos, articles, podcasts and more, and you can bookmark your favorites.
   - Website: Cosmos Education https://education.cosmosmagazine.com/

5. The British Antarctic Survey (BAS):
- BAS provides educational resources, research findings, and information on Antarctic science and conservation efforts, including materials for teachers and students.
- Website: British Antarctic Survey

6. National Geographic Education:
- National Geographic offers educational resources on polar environments, climate change, and conservation, including articles, videos, and lesson plans for teachers.
- Website: National Geographic Education
  https://www.nationalgeographic.org/education

7. Palmer Station Antarctica Resources
- Data nuggets about penguins, lesson ideas, live webcams, real-time research, resources for students and families, and even the possibility of chatting with scientists stationed at Palmer Station are included within the unique education resources found here.
- Website: Palmer Station Antarctica LTER
  https://pallter.marine.rutgers.edu/education-outreach/resources/

8. National Science Foundation resources
- Videos about Antarctica, printables for teachers (including animal cards!) penguin science, printable posters, information about the research stations, images, infographics and more.
- Website: https://www.nsf.gov/focus-areas/arctic-antarctic/educational-resources#lessons-and-activities-467

9. **Antarctic Rights Alliance:**
*   The Antarctic Rights Alliance is a group of people and organizations who believe that Antarctica should be protected, not just as a place for science, but as a living system with its own rights. They work to make sure Antarctica stays peaceful, untouched by mining or drilling, and safe for all the animals that call it home.

Instead of thinking about Antarctica as something humans can own or use, they want the world to see it as a unique, wild place that deserves care, respect, and a voice. Their goal? To create stronger protections now and for the future.
Website: antarcticrights.org

10. **Online Courses and Webinars:**
*   Various organizations, including the PEI and NSIDC, offer online courses and webinars focusing on polar literacy, climate change, and environmental education. These can provide educators with the latest research and teaching strategies. Coursera and EdX also offer courses about different aspects of Antarctica.

Experiment links:

*   **Water Density Experiment**

Science at home from the NC Museum of Natural Science:
https://naturalsciences.org/calendar/news/science-at-home-water-density-experiment/

*   **Melting Ice Experiment**

NASA's Jet Propulsion Lab provides a simple experiment for students to predict, observe, and compare melt rates of ice under different temperature conditions and in different solutions.
https://www.jpl.nasa.gov/edu/resources/lesson-plan/melting-ice-experiment/

Echoes from the Ice: Glossary

Adventure: An exciting journey where you discover new things or places.
Antarctic Treaty: An agreement between countries to keep Antarctica peaceful, used for science and protected from harm.
Bioluminescence: When a living creature gives off light (like glowing krill!)
Bustling: Full of busy movement, sounds, and energy, even a wild place like Antarctica can be bustling with life!
Caldera: A big volcanic crater that forms when the top of a volcano collapses
Calving: When a chunk of ice breaks off a glacier, ice shelf, or even an iceberg, and crashes into the sea.
Climate: The usual weather in a place over many years.
Drake Passage: The stormy stretch of ocean between South America and Antarctica.
Ecosystem: A community where animals, plants, and their environment all work together to survive.
Encounter: To meet or come across something, often unexpectedly
Expedition: A special trip or journey with a goal, like exploring or doing science.
Fluke: The wide, flat tail of a whale, which helps it swim and dive.
Frigid: Very, very cold!
Fluttered: Moved quickly and lightly, like a bird's wings or snowflakes in the wind.
Glacier: A huge, slow-moving sheet of ice that shapes the land.
Groan: A deep, low sound, like the ice or sea might make when it shifts or moves.

Guardian: Someone (or something) that protects and watches over others or the Earth.

Habitat: The natural home of an animal or plant.

Ice: Frozen water found all over Antarctica in glaciers, icebergs, and sea ice.

Ice shelf: A thick sheet of ice that floats on the ocean but is still connected to land.

Iceberg: A giant chunk of ice that has broken off a glacier or ice shelf and floats in the ocean.

Jagged: Rough, uneven, and pointy, like the edge of broken ice or sharp rocks.

Krill: Tiny shrimp-like animals that are super important in the Antarctic food chain. Whales, penguins, seabirds, and seals eat them, among others.

Lingered: Stayed in one place longer than expected.

Molted / Moulted: When animals shed old skin, feathers, or fur to make way for new ones.

Nutrients: Tiny things in food or water that help living things grow and stay healthy.

Ocean: A huge body of salt water that covers most of Earth; Antarctica is surrounded by the Southern Ocean.

Parka: A thick, warm coat used in freezing places like Antarctica.

Penguin: A flightless bird that swims in the ocean and waddles on land, there are 18 species in the world but only a few species live in Antarctica!
Phytoplankton: Tiny plant-like organisms that float in the ocean and make food from sunlight. They help feed the whole food web!
Porpoised: When an animal (like a penguin or dolphin) jumps in and out of the water while swimming.
Regurgitating: When an animal brings food back up in their throat; penguin parents do this to feed their chicks.
Ripples: Small waves or movements on the surface of water, or even in the air.
Salps: Clear, jelly-like animals that drift through the sea and filter tiny bits of food.
Sea: A smaller part of the ocean; cold seas surround Antarctica.
Seal: A sea mammal that can swim in icy water and rest on ice or land.
Ship: A large boat used for traveling long distances; Alexandra took one to Antarctica!
Spyhopping: When a whale pops its head out of the water to look around.
Treaty: A big agreement between countries
Ushuaia: The southernmost city in the world, located in Argentina. It's where Alexandra began her journey to Antarctica.
Whale: A giant sea mammal; many species live near Antarctica and eat krill.

Words Of The Ice Guardian For Young Protectors

These are the quiet messages and powerful reminders whispered throughout Alexandra's journey. Each one is a call to notice, remember, and protect the frozen world of Antarctica and all the life it holds.

Listen well.

The cold wind carries more than just snow. It carries stories. Be the one who listens.

Notice what others miss.

A krill, a glimmer in the ice, a shift in the water. The smallest things matter most.

Even the smallest actions create ripples.

What you do—how you speak, what you share, how you care—reaches farther than you know.

Protect what you can.

You don't have to save the whole world. Start with what's around you.

That is enough.

Speak for the silent.

The penguins, the whales, the ice itself—they can't tell their stories.

But you can.

You are the storyteller.

This is your notebook now. Use your words to open eyes, stir hearts,

and inspire action.

You are not alone.

Every ripple joins another. There are others—storykeepers, explorers, protectors—just like you.

Remember.

This place is fragile. This moment is real. Carry it with you. Pass it on.

From the wind-carved cliffs of Deception Island to the deep waters where whales rise, the Ice Guardian reminds us: Wonder leads to wisdom. And wisdom leads to action.

Keep listening. Keep writing. Keep protecting.

www.ingramcontent.com/pod-product-compliance
Lightning Source LLC
Chambersburg PA
CBHW042023150426
43198CB00002B/45